The Internet

Andy Croft

Published in association with The Basic Skills Agency

Hodder & Stoughton

A MEMBER OF THE HODDER HEADLINE GROUP

Acknowledgements

Cover: Jacey (Debut Art)/Telegraph Colour Library

Photos: pp. 2, 20 © Reuters NewMedia Inc./Corbis; p 6 © Neil Munns/The Press Association Ltd; p 9 © Dennis Degnan/Corbis; p 12 © Associated Press AP; p 17 © Neil Munns/'PA' Photos; p 23 © Inge Yspeert/Corbis

Every effort has been made to trace copyright holders of material reproduced in this book. Any rights not acknowledged will be acknowledged in subsequent printings if notice is given to the publisher.

Orders: please contact Bookpoint Ltd, 78 Milton Park, Abingdon, Oxon OX14 4TD. Telephone (44) 01235 827720, Fax: (44) 01235 400454. Lines are open from 9.00–6.00, Monday to Saturday, with a 24 hour message answering service. Email address: orders@bookpoint.co.uk

British Library Cataloguing in Publication Data
A catalogue record for this title is available from The British Library

ISBN 0 340 80069 0

First published 2001
Impression number   10 9 8 7 6 5 4 3 2 1
Year   2007 2006 2005 2004 2003 2002 2001

Copyright © 2001 Andy Croft

Typeset by SX Composing DTP, Rayleigh, Essex
Printed in Great Britain for Hodder & Stoughton Educational, a division of Hodder Headline Plc, 338 Euston Road, London NW1 3BH by Redwood Books, Trowbridge, Wilts.

Contents

The Internet

It's amazing.
It's beautiful.
It's simple.
It's clever.
It's fascinating.
It's useful.
It's incredible.
It's scary.

It's hard to understand.
It's hard to explain.

You can't touch it.
You can't hold it.
You can't eat it.
You can't smell it.
But it's everywhere.

It's the future.

It's the Internet.

The internet allows you to see and talk to someone from the other side of the world.

1 Beginnings

It all began in the 1950s and 1960s.
America and Russia
were preparing for a nuclear war.
They knew millions of people would die.
But they wanted their computers to survive.
The Americans started connecting
their computers together.
By doing this, if one computer
was destroyed in a war,
then all the information would be saved.

In the 1970s scientists and universities
got together.
They set up their own computer networks.
In the 1980s big businesses joined in.

In 1989 a British engineer
had a brilliant idea.
His name was Tim Berners-Lee.
He wanted a world-wide network of computers.
This way scientists could share their ideas.

The Internet was born.

Soon everyone wanted to join in.
In 1993 there were just one million people
connected to the Internet.
Today there are over 400 million people
on-line!

2   Caught in the Net

On the Internet
you can do all kinds of things.

You can do any of the following.
- Play games.
- Go shopping.
- Buy tickets for a concert.
- Hear the latest news.
- Make friends.
- Watch films.
- Book a holiday.
- Check your bank account.
- Find out what's happening
  at your football club.
- Visit an art gallery.
- Send an e-mail.
- Read a newspaper.
- Listen to music.
- Buy books.
- Visit a museum.
- Join a discussion.
- Get help with your homework.

You can even find out which
celebrity would be your ideal partner!

NetAid was one of the first concerts that could be seen live over the Internet.

You can start your own web-site.

And all it usually costs
is the price of a local phone call!

You can find out about anything you want
on the Internet.
But can you guess the most visited web-sites
on the net?

Pokemon,
Britney Spears,
Dragonball
and WWF wrestling . . .

3 What is the Internet?

The Internet connects computers
all over the world.
It is sometimes called
the World Wide Web.
That's why all computer addresses
begin 'www'.

How do you go on the Internet?
All you need is a telephone
and a computer with a modem.
The modem turns words and pictures
into sounds.
The sounds are carried down the telephone.
At the other end they are turned back
into words and pictures.
You also need an ISP
(Internet Service Provider) disk
to link up with the net.

The Internet allows you to access all sorts of information.

No one owns the Internet.
No one controls it.
No one knows how big it is.
It just keeps on growing.
There are one-and-a-half billion pages
on the Internet.
There are over 350 million pictures.
Every day another three million pages
are added.

The Internet is like a weird library.
Imagine millions and millions of books
in a huge pile on the floor.
You can read any book you want.
But where do you start?

4   Surfing

There are two ways of finding what you want
on the Internet.

The first way is to use a web-site address.
Remember to type the address carefully.
For example, Britney Spears'
Internet address is:
http://www.britneyspears.com
If you make one small mistake
you won't get through.

The second way is to use a search engine.
You can use a search engine if you don't
know the site address.
Just type in a word or a name
next to the 'Search' box on the screen.
Searching is easy –
but finding what you want
can take a long time.

DotComGuy spent a year living with only the Internet. All his food and supplies were ordered online.

Imagine you are a football fan.
You want to catch up with
your favourite team.
Just type in the name.
A list of useful web-sites
will appear on the screen.
There's only one problem.
There are probably hundreds
of web-sites about your club.
Some of them will be very useful.
But not all of them.

So how do you know which web-site to open?
You just have to pick one.
Perhaps you will find what you want
straight away.
If you don't find what you want,
just go back to the list
and pick another site.
Or click on any words that are underlined.
This is called hypertext.
It will take you on to another page
or another site.
If you don't find what you want there,
just keep moving on.

You are now surfing the Internet!

5   e-mail

Today there are almost one billion
e-mail boxes around the world.

Sending e-mail is easy.
Just type your message and press 'Send'.
It's a lot quicker than posting a letter.
You might get a reply
in less than five minutes.
You can also send photographs or pictures.

People who write a lot of e-mails
sometimes write in a special code.
It saves time if you are very busy.

One code makes words out of letters
on the keyboard.
Look on page 16 for some examples.

BBL	=	Be back later
CYA	=	See ya
CUL8R	=	See you later
GDM8	=	G'day mate
GR8	=	Great
PBT	=	Pay back time
UR	=	You are

Some of these code words are called smileys.
They are made by pressing
some of the other keys:

\o/	=	Someone cheering!!

Here are some more smileys.
Turn the page sideways.
Can you see the cartoon faces?

:-)	=	Happy
:-(	=	Sad
:-D	=	Laughing
:-o	=	Shocked
:8)	=	Pig
0:-)	=	Angel
}:>	=	Devil

You can contact people all over the world using the Internet.

6 www.completely barmy

The Internet is an amazing place.
But it is also a bit strange sometimes.

There are thousands of crazy web-sites:

- Tasty Insect Recipes.
- I Can Eat Glass.
- The Joy of Socks.
- The Ants are My Friends.
- 99 Ways to Open a Beer Bottle!

There are sites about aliens,
fairies and vampires.
There are sites about paintings
by dogs and cats.
There are sites about talking to hamsters
or being sick.

Junk e-mail on your computer is called spam.

A 'hacker' is someone who
breaks into computers for fun.
A 'cracker' is someone who
breaks into computers to steal information.
'Cyborgs' work all day on the computer.
Then they come home and play on it too.

Computers can catch diseases
on the Internet.
These are called computer viruses.
A few years ago millions of people found a love-letter
in their e-mail.
It said 'I Love You' on the outside.
Everyone opened the letter.
Inside was a deadly computer virus.
It destroyed all their files!

Someone even managed to hack into the White House computer systems.

In 1997 members of a top US web-design team
were excited.
They thought aliens were sending them messages
on the net.
The aliens promised to take them
up in their space-ship.
But they said the designers
must leave their bodies behind.
So everyone in the team killed themselves.

7   Into Cyber Space

The Internet is everywhere.
People use the Internet
in offices and in shops.
They use it in museums, in libraries,
in schools and at home.
There are even cyber cafés
where you can surf the net
while you eat.

(What do you eat in a cyber café?
Answer: Microchips!)

You can connect to the net using
lap-tops, PCs or even mobile phones.
You can connect to the net
on a plane or on a ship.
You can connect to the net
in a hot-air balloon.
You can even connect to the net
if you are in outer space.
When the Pathfinder space-probe landed
on Mars, millions of people watched
live on the Internet.

You can eat whilst you surf in cyber cafés.

You can be married on the Internet.
You can be buried on the Internet.
Pop stars put songs on the net
before they are in the shops.
The Pope has a web-site.
The Queen has a web-site.
Presidents and Prime Ministers
answer questions on the Internet.
There has even been
an Internet bank-robbery!

No one knows for sure
what the Internet will do next.
Maybe your fridge will order food on the net
when it is empty.
Perhaps your washing machine will e-mail
the plumber
when it needs a spare part.

US citizens spend five per cent
of their lives on the Internet.
By the year 2005 there will be
800 million people on the net.
That's a lot of people.

But there are over six *billion* people
on the planet.
Most are too poor to ever use the Internet.
Half the people on earth
have never even used a telephone.

Some Useful Words

Boot up   To start your computer.

Blog   Your own personal web-site.

Download   Copying part of a web-site
onto your computer from the net.

Eye-candy   Graphics that make a web-site
look interesting.

FAQ   The most frequently
asked questions
on a web-site.

GIF/JPG   Graphic image files.

Hits   The number of people
who visit a web-site.

Hyperlink   Words or pictures
you can click on
to go to another page or web-site.

ISP   Internet Service Provider.

Logging on	Connecting to the net.
MP3	A compressed music format.
MPG	A file that can carry video film.
Newbies	Newcomers to the net or a web-site.
On line	When your computer is connected to the net.
Search engine	Helps you find what you are looking for on the net.
URL	A web-address.
Webmaster	Someone who designs web-sites.
Zip files	Files that can carry a lot of information without using too much room on your computer.